# The Man in the Moon As He Sails the Sky
## AND OTHER MOON VERSE

Collected and Illustrated by
Ann Schweninger

DODD, MEAD & COMPANY * NEW YORK

I wish to extend special thanks to Ivan Schweninger
and Donna Brooks for their assistance in collecting
the verse.                                        —A.S.

Grateful acknowledgment is made to the authors, agents, and publishers of the following
material for permission to reprint:

"Halloween Song" by Marjorie Barrows. The first stanza is reprinted with permission
of the author.

"The Moon's the North Wind's Cooky," "What the Gray-Winged Fairy Said," and "What
the Snow Man Said," by Vachel Lindsay. Reprinted with permission of Macmillan
Publishing Co., Inc., from *Collected Poems* by Vachel Lindsay, copyright 1914 by Macmillan
Publishing Co., Inc. Copyright renewed 1942 by Elizabeth C. Lindsay.

"Autumn" by T.E. Hulme, from *Speculations* by T.E. Hulme, published in Great Britain by
Routledge & Kegan Paul Ltd., and in the United States by Harcourt Brace Jovanovich, Inc.

"Early Morning" by Hilaire Belloc, from *Sonnets and Verse* by Hilaire Belloc, published by
Gerald Duckworth & Co., Ltd. Reprinted by permission of A.D. Peters & Co., Ltd.

Library of Congress Cataloging in Publication Data
Main entry under title:

The Man in the Moon as he sails the sky
and other moon verse.

SUMMARY: Poems about the moon from such sources as
Mother Goose, Vachel Lindsay, Edward Lear, William
Wordsworth, and R. L. Stevenson.

1. Moon—Juvenile poetry.   2. Children's poetry.
[1. Moon—Poetry.   2. Poetry—Collections]
I. Schweninger, Ann.
PN6110.M6M3        821.008 032        79-52051
ISBN 0-396-07741-2

To Uri Shulevitz

The Man in the Moon as he sails the sky
Is a very remarkable skipper,
But he made a mistake when he tried to take
A drink of milk from the Dipper.

He dipped right out of the Milky Way
And slowly and carefully filled it;
The Big Bear growled, and the Little Bear howled
And frightened him so that he spilled it!

Three little witches
   Pranced in the garden,
Three little witches
   Danced from the moon;
One wore a wishing hat,
One held a pussy-cat,
One went a-pitty-pat
   And whispered a tune.

There was an old woman tossed up in a basket,
　　Seventeen times as high as the moon;
And where she was going, I couldn't but ask it,
　　For in her hand she carried a broom.
Old woman, old woman, old woman, quoth I,
　　O whither, O whither, O whither so high?
To sweep the cobwebs off the sky!
　　Shall I go with you? Aye, by-and-by.

The Moon's a snowball. See the drifts
Of white that cross the sphere.
The Moon's a snowball, melted down
A dozen times a year.

On Saturday night I lost my wife,
And where do you think I found her?
Up in the moon, singing a tune,
And all the stars around her.

The moon shines bright,
The stars give a light,
You may play at any game
At ten o'clock at night.

*H*ey diddle, diddle,

  The cat and the fiddle,

The cow jumped over the moon;

  The little dog laughed

  To see such fun,

And the dish ran away with

  the spoon.

There was a maid on Scrabble Hill,
And if not dead, she lives there still.
She grew so tall, she reached the sky,
And on the moon, hung clothes to dry.

The Moon's the North Wind's cooky.
He bites it, day by day,
Until there's but a rim of scraps
That crumble all away.

The South Wind is a baker.
He kneads clouds in his den,
And bakes a crisp new moon *that . . . greedy*
*North . . . Wind . . . eats . . . again!*

What's the news of the day,
Good neighbor, I pray?
They say a balloon
Is gone up to the moon.

*T*here was an old person
  of Skye,
Who waltzed with a
  Bluebottle fly!
They buzz'd a sweet tune
  to the light of the moon,
And entranced all the
  people of Skye.

Tonight the color
Of the moon
Is amber tea
In a silver spoon.

*A* touch of cold in the Autumn night
  I walked abroad,
  And saw the ruddy moon lean over a hedge
  Like a red-faced farmer.
  I did not stop to speak, but nodded;
  And round about were the wistful stars
  With white faces like town children.

Girls and boys, come out to play,

The moon is shining bright as day.

Leave your supper, and leave your sleep,

And come with your playfellows into the street.

Come with a whoop, come with a call,

Come with a good will or not at all.

Up the ladder and down the wall,

A halfpenny roll will serve us all;

You find milk, and I'll find flour,

And we'll have a pudding in half-an-hour.

Moon, moon,
    Mak' me a pair o' shoon,
    And I'll dance till you be done.

The moon's a gong, hung in the wild,
Whose song the fays hold dear.
Of course you do not hear it, child.
It takes a *fairy* ear.

The full moon is a splendid gong
That beats as night grows still.
It sounds above the evening song
Of dove or whippoorwill.

The moon on the one hand, the dawn on the other:
The moon is my sister, the dawn is my brother.
The moon on my left and the dawn on my right.
My brother, good morning: my sister, good night.

There's something in a flying horse,
There's something in a huge balloon;
But through the clouds I'll never float
Until I have a little boat,
Shaped like the crescent-moon.

The moon has a face like a clock in the hall;
She shines on thieves on the garden wall,
On streets and fields and harbor quays,
And birdies asleep in the forks of the trees.

The squalling cat and the sneaking mouse,
The howling dog by the door of the house,
The bat that lies in bed at noon,
All love to be out by the light of the moon.

But all things that belong to the day
Cuddle to sleep to be out of her way;
And flowers and children close their eyes
Till up in the morning the sun shall rise.

*I* see the moon,

    And the moon sees me;

God bless the moon,

    And God bless me.

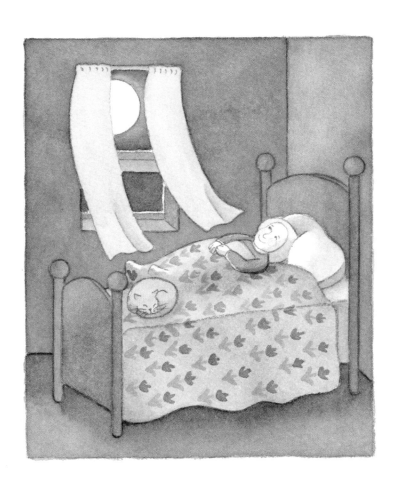

## DATE DUE

| AUG 20 '90 | | | |
|---|---|---|---|
| | | | |
| | | | |
| | | | |
| | | | |
| | | | |
| | | | |
| | | | |
| | | | |
| | | | |
| | | | |
| | | | |
| | | | |
| | | | |
| | | | |
| | | | |
| | | | |
| GAYLORD | | | PRINTED IN U.S.A. |